The Tell-Tale Heart

*A Harrowing Confession of Guilt,
Paranoia & the Unbearable Weight of
a Beating Secret*

A Modern Translation
Adapted for the Contemporary Reader

Edgar Allan Poe

Translated by Tim Zengerink

Table of Contents

Preface
Message to the Reader

Rebuilding the Greatest Library in Human History

Thousands of years ago, the Library of Alexandria was the heart of global knowledge — a sanctuary where the wisdom of every known civilization was gathered and shared freely.

And then, it was lost.

Now, we're rebuilding it — and you are invited to join us.

At the Library of Alexandria, we've set out to make every book available to every person on Earth — not just in print, but in every language, every format, and for every reader.

Here's how we do it:

- **Deluxe Print Editions at True Printing Cost** - Order any book as a high-quality paperback, elegant hardcover, or stunning boxset — and only pay what it costs to print. No markups. No middlemen.
- **Unlimited Access to the Greatest Works** - Enjoy thousands of timeless classics — from Plato to Shakespeare to Tolstoy — in beautiful, modern eBook and audiobook editions. Read and listen without limits — for every reader, everywhere.
- **Modern Translations for Every Language & Dialect** - We're reimagining the classics in clear, accessible language — and translating them into every dialect imaginable. Everyone deserves to understand humanity's greatest ideas.

When you visit **LibraryofAlexandria.com**, you're not just accessing books — you're joining a global movement to restore, preserve, and share the wisdom of civilization.

Join us today at LibraryofAlexandria.com

Together, we'll ensure the light of human wisdom never fades again.

With gratitude,

The Modern Library of Alexandria Team

Visit:
www.libraryofalexandria.com
Or scan the code below:

Introduction

A Descent into Madness: Poe's Window into the Unstable Mind

Few literary works plunge the reader so directly and unrelentingly into the heart of madness as Edgar Allan Poe's The Tell-Tale Heart. First published in 1843, this brief but electrifying tale has earned its place among the most enduring psychological horror stories ever written. It is a masterclass in suspense, unreliable narration, and the terrifying power of guilt. But it is also much more: a philosophical meditation on the fragility of reason, the complexity of human motivation, and the darkness that lurks in the recesses of the mind.

The plot is deceptively simple. A nameless narrator insists, with increasing fervor, that he is sane—even as he describes the calculated murder of an old man with a "vulture eye," the concealment of the corpse beneath floorboards, and the eventual unraveling of his composure as he imagines (or perhaps hears) the ghostly heartbeat of his victim pounding beneath the floor. In fewer than two thousand words, Poe crafts an experience that is not just read, but felt—a crescendo of tension, dread, and psychological collapse.

What gives this story its enduring power is not just its suspenseful narrative, but its innovative structure and voice. From the first sentence—"True!—nervous—very, very dreadfully nervous I had been and am; but why will you say that I am mad?"—the reader is pulled into a monologue of defensive hysteria, a spiraling attempt to rationalize the irrational. The narrator's voice is manic, compelling, intimate, and deeply disturbing. He is not telling a story; he is pleading a case, performing a confession disguised as a justification. This direct address makes us complicit. We are not just observers—we are witnesses, judges, and perhaps, in the narrator's mind, accomplices.

Poe's innovation in this story lies in his exploration of the first-person unreliable narrator. Rather than presenting a moralistic tale in which the wicked are punished and the good are rewarded, Poe presents a character whose guilt and madness are indistinguishable. The horror is not found in the crime itself, but in the psychological aftermath. It is not the murder that destroys the narrator—it is his own conscience.

Through this lens, The Tell-Tale Heart becomes not just a tale of murder, but a profound investigation of guilt as a universal and destabilizing force. The beating heart is both literal and symbolic: a manifestation of the narrator's suppressed remorse, his internalized fear, and the unbearable truth that crimes of the soul cannot be buried. In this way, Poe elevates horror into the realm of existential inquiry.

Guilt as the Ultimate Haunting: The Sound Beneath the Floorboards

To fully appreciate The Tell-Tale Heart, it is important to understand how Poe manipulates time, sound, and sensory perception to create a psychological landscape more terrifying than any physical setting. The entire story takes place in a liminal space: somewhere between confession and madness, between past action and present obsession, between real sound and imagined echoes. The narrator insists on his sanity, but the very structure of his storytelling betrays him. His timeline is erratic, his details obsessive, and his voice riddled with inconsistencies. This instability becomes the ground upon which the reader must try to balance.

Central to this story is the old man's "vulture eye"—a feature that the narrator describes as being so disturbing that it compels him to commit murder. But why the eye? Why not hatred of the old man himself? Why not money, revenge, or passion? Poe's genius lies in leaving this ambiguous. The eye becomes a symbol—a disturbing image that represents surveillance, vulnerability, judgment, or the presence of a truth the narrator cannot bear to face. The eye looks into him, and in looking, unmasks him. The crime is not merely an act of violence—it is an attempt to destroy that which sees too clearly.

Yet even after the eye is closed forever, the crime does not relieve the narrator. Instead of peace, he is haunted by sound—the imagined thudding of a heart that should no longer beat. Here, Poe transforms the heartbeat from a biological rhythm into a spiritual metronome, measuring out the narrator's descent into guilt. The sound is subjective, heard only by him, but it gains a terrifying realism. It is a manifestation of internal judgment, a ghost of conscience louder than any judge or jury.

This sound, which rises and swells in the final paragraphs, mirrors the narrator's rising panic. Poe's syntax quickens, his punctuation fragments, and the repetition becomes a drumbeat of its own. "Louder!—louder!—louder!" the narrator cries, until he can no longer bear the weight of his own guilt. The final confession—"I admit the deed!—tear up the planks! here, here!—It is the beating of his hideous heart!"—is not an act of redemption, but of

4

psychological implosion. Guilt, unchecked, has destroyed the narrator from within.

Here, Poe reveals that the truest punishment for crime is not always external—it is internal, inescapable, and often self-inflicted. In a society where justice might be flawed or absent, conscience becomes the final tribunal. And in The Tell-Tale Heart, conscience is a voice that cannot be silenced.

Poe's Legacy and the Birth of Psychological Horror

Edgar Allan Poe is widely credited as one of the founding figures of modern horror and detective fiction. But his contributions go beyond genre innovation. He was a literary architect of the human psyche—mapping madness, obsession, and inner torment long before the disciplines of psychology and psychiatry had formal names for these conditions. The Tell-Tale Heart exemplifies this approach. It is not a story about murder—it is a story about a mind in collapse.

By placing the reader inside the mind of a murderer, Poe challenges the Victorian moral framework that so often dominated literature in his time. There is no omniscient narrator guiding us toward ethical conclusions. Instead, we are submerged in subjectivity, left to sort through madness and motive ourselves. This interiority would become a hallmark of later literary movements, including modernism, existentialism, and psychological realism. Writers like Dostoevsky, Kafka, and Faulkner would build on this foundation, crafting narrators whose inner voices were often more terrifying than any external danger.

In addition, The Tell-Tale Heart laid the groundwork for the modern horror genre's preoccupation with the mind. The haunted house would become less important than the haunted brain. Monsters would be replaced by madness. The question would shift from "What lurks in the dark?" to "What lurks in me?" Horror would become introspective, metaphysical, and philosophical.

Poe's mastery also lies in his compression. Unlike gothic novels of the 18th century, which spanned hundreds of pages and intricate plots, Poe condensed terror into the short story form. Every word counts. Every sentence builds pressure. This economy of language gives The Tell-Tale Heart its explosive power. It is not meant to be read slowly and analyzed in parts—it is meant to be inhaled, experienced, and survived.

In the classroom, The Tell-Tale Heart has become a staple of literary study. It invites discussion on narrative technique, symbolism, unreliable narration, and the interplay between mental illness and morality. In popular culture, the story has inspired countless adaptations, films, references, and reinterpretations. Its legacy endures not because of its plot, but because of its insight. It asks us to consider how thin the line is between rationality and madness, between guilt and justice, between silence and confession.

To read The Tell-Tale Heart is to journey into the dark mirror of our own moral boundaries. It does not offer easy answers. It forces us to listen—to the voice that insists it is sane, and to the heartbeat that will not stop. And as the story closes, the echo lingers. In the silence that follows the final sentence, we too may hear a sound beneath the floorboards—not from the page, but from our own sense of right and wrong, our own hidden fears, our own tell-tale hearts.

The Tell-Tale Heart

Yes!—anxious—extremely, extremely terrifyingly anxious I had been and still am; but why do you insist that I am insane? The illness had heightened my senses—not destroyed—not weakened them. Most of all, my sense of hearing was sharp. I heard everything in heaven and on earth. I heard countless things in hell. How, then, can I be insane? Listen! and notice how clearly—how peacefully I can tell you the entire story.

I can't explain how the idea first came into my mind, but once it took hold, it consumed my thoughts both day and night. There was no specific goal behind it. There was no emotion driving it. I cared for the old man. He had never done anything wrong to me. He had never offended me. I didn't want his money. I believe it was his eye! Yes, that was it! He had an eye like a vulture's—a pale blue eye with a cloudy film covering it. Every time he looked at me, my blood turned ice cold; and so slowly—very slowly—I decided to end the old man's life, and in doing so, free myself from that eye once and for all.

Now here's the thing. You think I'm crazy. Crazy people don't know anything. But you should have seen me. You should have seen how cleverly I went about it—with what care—with what planning—with what deception I worked! I was never nicer to the old man than during that entire week before I killed him. And every night, around midnight, I turned the handle of his door and opened it— oh, so quietly! And then, when I had created an opening big enough for my head, I put in a dark lantern, completely closed, closed so that no light came out, and then I pushed in my head. Oh, you would have laughed to see how slyly I pushed it in! I moved it slowly—very, very slowly, so that I wouldn't wake the old man from his sleep. It took me an hour to get my whole head through the opening far enough that I could see him as he lay on his bed. Ha!—would a crazy person have been so clever as this? And then, when my head was well inside the room, I opened the lantern carefully—oh, so carefully—carefully (because the hinges squeaked)—I opened it just enough that a single thin beam fell on the vulture eye. And this I did for seven long nights—every night right at midnight—but I found the eye always shut; and so it was impossible to do the deed; because it wasn't the old man who bothered me, but his Evil Eye. And every morning, when daybreak came, I went boldly into the room, and spoke confidently to him, calling him by name in a cheerful voice, and asking how he had spent the night. So you see he would have had to be a very wise old man, indeed, to suspect that every night, right at twelve o'clock, I looked in on him while he slept.

On the eighth night, I was even more careful than usual when opening the door. The minute hand of a watch moves faster than I moved that night. I had never before felt the full extent of my abilities—my cleverness. I could barely control my sense of victory. Just imagine—there I was, slowly opening the door bit by bit, while he had no idea about my secret actions or thoughts. I almost laughed out loud at the thought, and maybe he heard me because he suddenly shifted in his bed, as though something had alarmed him. You might think I stepped back—but I didn't. His room was completely dark, pitch black, since the shutters were tightly closed to keep out thieves, so I knew he couldn't see the door opening. I continued pushing it open slowly, steadily.

I had my head inside, and was just about to open the lantern, when my thumb slipped on the metal clasp, and the old man jumped up in bed, shouting—"Who's there?"

I remained completely motionless and stayed silent. For an entire hour I didn't move at all, and during that time I couldn't hear him lying down. He was still sitting upright in his bed, listening—exactly as I had done, night after night, paying attention to the death-watch beetles ticking in the wall.

Soon I heard a faint groan, and I recognized it as the groan of deadly fear. It wasn't a groan of pain or sorrow—absolutely not!—it was the quiet, muffled sound that rises from the depths of the soul when overwhelmed with terror. I knew that sound well. Many nights, right at midnight, when everyone in the world was asleep, it had risen from my own chest, intensifying with its terrible echo the fears that tormented me. I tell you I knew it well. I understood what the old man was feeling, and I felt sorry for him, even though I quietly laughed inside. I knew that he had been lying awake ever since the first small sound, when he had shifted in his bed. His fears had been building up inside him ever since. He had been trying to convince himself they were groundless, but he couldn't. He had been telling himself—"It's nothing but the wind in the chimney—it's just a mouse running across the floor," or "It's simply a cricket that chirped once." Yes, he had been trying to reassure himself with these explanations: but he had discovered it was all useless. All useless; because Death, while approaching him had crept forward with his dark shadow ahead of him, and surrounded his victim. And it was the sorrowful power of that unseen shadow that made him sense—even though he couldn't see or hear anything—sense the presence of my head inside the room.

When I had waited for a long time, very patiently, without hearing him lie down, I decided to open a small crack—a very, very small crack in the lantern. So I opened it—you can't imagine how carefully, carefully—until finally a single dim beam, like a spider's thread, shot out from the crack and landed directly on the vulture eye.

The eye was open—completely, utterly open—and rage consumed me as I stared at it. I could see it with absolute clarity—entirely a dull blue color, covered by a revolting film that froze the very core of my being; yet I couldn't make out any other part of the old man's face or body: I had aimed the light beam instinctively, focusing it exactly on that cursed eye.

Haven't I already explained to you that what you think is madness is actually just my senses being extremely sharp? Well, at that moment, I heard a quiet, muffled, rapid sound in my ears, like the ticking of a watch wrapped in cotton. I recognized that sound immediately. It was the old man's heartbeat. This sound made my rage grow stronger, just like how the beating of a drum fills a soldier with courage.

But still I held back and remained motionless. I barely drew breath. I kept the lantern perfectly still. I tested how steadily I could keep the beam focused on the eye. Meanwhile the demonic drumming of the heart grew stronger. It became faster and faster, and more thunderous with each passing second. The old man's fear must have reached its peak! It became more thunderous, I tell you, more deafening each moment!—are you listening carefully? I have mentioned that I am on edge: indeed I am. And now in the dead of night, surrounded by the terrible quiet of that ancient house, such an unusual sound filled me with overwhelming dread. Still, for several more minutes I held back and remained frozen. But the pounding became more thunderous, more deafening! I believed the heart would explode. And then a fresh worry gripped me—the noise might reach a neighbor! The old man's time had arrived! With a piercing scream, I flung open the lantern and lunged into the room. He cried out once—just once. In a flash I yanked him to the ground, and dragged the massive bed on top of him. I then grinned cheerfully, pleased to find the task nearly complete. But for several minutes, the heart continued beating with a dampened sound. This, though, did not trouble me; it could not be detected through the wall. Finally it stopped. The old man had died. I lifted the bed and inspected the body. Yes, he was cold, completely lifeless. I pressed my hand against the heart and kept it there for several minutes. There was no pulse. He was completely lifeless. His eye would never disturb me again.

If you still believe I'm insane, that opinion will change once I explain the careful steps I took to hide the body. As the night grew late, I worked quickly but quietly. First, I took the corpse apart. I severed the head, then the arms, and finally the legs.

I then removed three floorboards from the bedroom and placed everything between the wooden supports. I replaced the boards so skillfully and cleverly that no human eye—not even his—could have spotted anything amiss. There was nothing to clean up—no stain of any sort—no trace of blood whatsoever. I had been too careful for that. A container had caught it all—ha! ha!

When I finished these tasks, it was four o'clock—still as dark as midnight. As the bell rang the hour, someone knocked at the front door. I went downstairs to answer it feeling lighthearted—after all, what did I have to be afraid of now? Three men entered, introducing themselves with complete politeness as police officers. A neighbor had heard a scream during the night; this had raised suspicion that something terrible had happened; a report had been filed at the police station, and they had been assigned to search the house.

I smiled—what did I have to fear? I welcomed the gentlemen warmly. The scream, I explained, had been my own during a dream. The old man, I told them, was away in the countryside. I took my visitors throughout the entire house. I encouraged them to search—to search thoroughly. Eventually, I led them to his bedroom. I showed them his valuables, safe and untouched. In my overwhelming confidence, I brought chairs into the room and invited them to rest there from their exhausting work, while I myself, in the reckless boldness of my complete victory, positioned my own chair directly over the exact spot where the victim's body lay buried.

The officers were satisfied. My behavior had convinced them. I was remarkably calm. They sat down, and while I responded cheerfully, they talked about everyday matters. But before long, I felt myself growing pale and wanted them to leave. My head hurt, and I imagined a ringing in my ears: but they continued to sit and kept talking. The ringing became clearer:—it persisted and grew more distinct: I spoke more freely to eliminate the sensation: but it continued and became more defined—until, finally, I realized that the sound was not coming from inside my ears.

I'm sure I turned very pale at that moment, but I spoke more smoothly and with a louder voice. Still, the sound grew stronger—and what was I supposed to do? It was a quiet, muffled, rapid sound—exactly like the ticking of a watch wrapped in cotton. I struggled to breathe—yet the officers couldn't hear it. I spoke faster and with more intensity, but the noise kept getting louder. I stood up and started arguing about meaningless things, speaking in a high pitch with wild hand gestures, but the noise kept getting louder. Why wouldn't they just leave? I walked back and forth across the floor with heavy steps, as if the men's comments had driven me into a rage—but the noise kept getting louder. Oh God! What was I supposed to do? I was foaming at the mouth— I was ranting—I was cursing! I grabbed the chair I had been sitting on and scraped it across the floorboards, but the noise rose above everything else and kept growing louder. It became louder—louder—louder! And still the men continued their pleasant conversation and kept smiling. Could it be that they really couldn't hear it? Almighty God!—no, no! They could hear it!—they were suspicious!—they knew!—they were mocking my terror!— that's what I thought then, and that's what I think now. But anything would have been better than this torture! Anything would have been more bearable than this ridicule! I couldn't stand those fake smiles any longer! I felt like I had to scream or I would die! And then—once more!—listen! louder! louder! louder! louder!

"Criminals!" I screamed, "stop pretending! I confess to what I did—rip up the floorboards!—right here, right here!—It's the pounding of his terrible heart!"

Berenice

My companions told me that if I visited my beloved's
tomb, my sorrows would be somewhat lightened.
—Ebn Zaiat.

Misery comes in many forms. The suffering of our world
takes countless shapes. Stretching across the vast horizon
like a rainbow, its colors are as varied as those of that arc—
each one distinct, yet seamlessly woven together. Stretching
across the vast horizon like a rainbow! How is it that I have
drawn an image of ugliness from something beautiful?—
taken a symbol of sorrow from a promise of peace? But just
as, in moral philosophy, evil emerges from good, so in
reality, sorrow is born from joy. Either the memory of past
happiness becomes today's pain, or the suffering we
experience now stems from the bliss that could have been.

My baptismal name is Egaeus; I will not reveal my
family name. However, there are no towers in the land more
ancient and respected than my dark, gray, inherited halls.
Our family line has been known as a lineage of dreamers
and visionaries; and in many remarkable details—in the
nature of the family estate—in the frescoes of the main
hall—in the tapestries of the bedrooms—in the carved
stonework of some supports in the armory—but most
notably in the gallery of old paintings—in the design of the
library room—and, finally, in the very unusual nature of the
library's collection—there is more than enough proof to
support this belief.

My earliest memories are tied to that room and its
books—though I won't say more about those volumes. My

mother died there. I was born in that same place. But it's pointless to claim I hadn't lived before—that the soul doesn't have a prior existence. Do you disagree? Let's not debate it. I'm convinced of it myself, but I'm not trying to convince anyone else. There is, though, a memory of ghostly shapes—of spiritual and meaningful eyes—of sounds that were musical yet sorrowful—a memory that refuses to be pushed away; a recollection like a shadow—unclear, shifting, vague, unstable; and like a shadow too in how impossible it is for me to escape it as long as the sunlight of my reasoning mind continues to exist.

I was born in that room. Awakening from what felt like a long night of nonexistence—though it wasn't truly that—I found myself suddenly transported into the realm of fairy tales, into a palace built from imagination, into the untamed territories of scholarly contemplation and learning. It's not surprising that I looked around with shocked and passionate eyes, that I spent my childhood lost in books and wasted my youth lost in daydreams. What is surprising is that as the years passed and I reached the height of manhood while still living in my family's house, a remarkable stagnation settled over the vital forces of my life. It's amazing how completely my normal way of thinking became inverted. The real world began to affect me only as illusions and nothing more, while the fantastic ideas from the realm of dreams became not just the substance of my daily life, but actually became that life entirely and exclusively.

Berenice and I were cousins, and we grew up together in my father's house. But we developed very differently—I was sickly and consumed by darkness, while she was nimble, graceful, and bursting with vitality. She loved wandering the hillsides, while I preferred studying in solitude. I lived inside my own mind, completely devoted to the most intense and agonizing contemplation, while she moved through life without a care, never thinking about the shadows on her path or the silent passage of time. Berenice! I call out her name—Berenice! And from the gray ruins of memory, a thousand chaotic memories are awakened by that sound! How clearly I can see her now, just as she was in those early days of carefree happiness and joy! What magnificent yet otherworldly beauty! Like a spirit among the gardens of Arnheim! Like a water nymph by its fountains! And then— then everything becomes mystery and horror, a story that shouldn't be told. Disease—a deadly disease—struck her body like a desert wind, and even as I watched her, the force of change swept through her, affecting her mind, her habits, and her personality, and in the most subtle and terrifying way, even altering her very identity! The destroyer came and left, and the victim—where is she? I didn't recognize her anymore—or no longer knew her as Berenice.

Among the many illnesses that followed that devastating primary condition which brought about such a terrible transformation in both the moral and physical nature of my cousin, the most distressing and persistent was a form of epilepsy that often ended in a trance-like state—a trance that closely resembled actual death, and from which her recovery was usually shockingly sudden. Meanwhile, my own illness—for I have been told I should call it nothing else—my own illness grew rapidly worse and eventually took on the characteristics of an unusual and extraordinary type of obsession that gained strength by the hour and minute, ultimately achieving an incomprehensible control over me. This obsession, if I must call it that, involved an unhealthy oversensitivity of those mental faculties that metaphysical science calls attention. I probably won't be understood, but I'm afraid it's impossible to give the average reader an adequate sense of the intense nervous focus with which my powers of thought became completely absorbed in contemplating even the most common objects in the world.

To spend long, tireless hours lost in thought, with my focus completely captured by some trivial detail in the margin or in the printed text of a book; to become completely engrossed, for most of a summer day, in an unusual shadow cast diagonally across the tapestry or the floor; to lose myself for an entire night watching the constant flame of a lamp or the glowing coals of a fire; to spend whole days daydreaming about the fragrance of a flower; to repeat some ordinary word over and over again until the sound, through constant repetition, stopped carrying any meaning at all to the mind; to lose all awareness of movement or physical being through complete bodily stillness maintained for long periods with stubborn persistence: these were just a few of the most frequent and least harmful peculiarities brought on by a state of mental functioning that was not entirely without precedent, but certainly resisted any attempt at analysis or explanation.

Yet let me not be misunderstood. The excessive, intense, and unhealthy attention that trivial objects aroused in this way must not be confused with that reflective tendency common to all people, and especially indulged in by those with vivid imaginations. It was not even, as might be initially assumed, an extreme condition or exaggeration of such a tendency, but fundamentally and essentially distinct and different. In one case, the dreamer or enthusiast, being interested by an object that is usually not trivial, gradually loses sight of this object in a maze of deductions and suggestions arising from it, until, at the end of a daydream often filled with pleasure, he finds the starting point, or first cause of his thoughts, completely vanished and forgotten. In my case, the primary object was always trivial, although it took on, through my disturbed perception, a distorted and unreal importance. Few deductions, if any, were made; and those few stubbornly returned to the original object as a center. The meditations were never pleasurable; and, at the end of the reverie, the first cause, far from being out of sight, had gained that unnaturally exaggerated interest which was the defining characteristic of the disease. In short, the mental powers most particularly exercised were, with me, as I have said before, the attentive, and are, with the day-dreamer, the speculative.

My books during this time, while they may not have directly worsened my condition, clearly shared many of the same imaginative and disconnected qualities that characterized the disorder itself. I clearly recall, among others, the treatise by the distinguished Italian scholar Coelius Secundus Curio, "De Amplitudine Beati Regni Dei;" St. Augustine's masterwork, the "City of God;" and Tertullian's "De Carne Christi," in which the paradoxical statement "Mortuus est Dei filius; credible est quia ineptum est: et sepultus resurrexit; certum est quia impossibile est," consumed all of my attention for many weeks of intensive yet unproductive study.

Thus it became clear that, disturbed from its equilibrium only by minor matters, my reasoning resembled that ocean cliff described by Ptolemy Hephestion, which consistently withstood the assaults of human force and the more savage rage of waters and winds, yet trembled only at the touch of the flower known as Asphodel. And while, to a superficial observer, it might seem certain that the transformation caused by her tragic illness in Berenice's moral state would provide me with numerous subjects for that intense and unusual contemplation whose character I have taken considerable effort to describe, this was not at all the situation. During the clear periods of my affliction, her misfortune did indeed cause me anguish, and deeply feeling the complete destruction of her beautiful and kind existence, I regularly reflected, often and with bitterness, on the miraculous forces by which such an extraordinary change had been so suddenly accomplished. However, these thoughts did not share the peculiar nature of my condition, and were the kind that would have occurred, under comparable circumstances, to ordinary people in general. Faithful to its own nature, my disorder delighted in the less significant but more shocking alterations created in Berenice's physical form—in the strange and most horrifying transformation of her personal identity.

During the peak of her extraordinary beauty, I certainly had never loved her. In the peculiar contradiction of my existence, my emotions had never originated from the heart, and my desires always stemmed from the mind. Through the gray light of early morning—among the latticed shadows of the forest at midday—and in the quiet of my library at night—she had passed before my eyes, and I had observed her—not as the living and breathing Berenice, but as the Berenice of a dream; not as a creature of the earth, earthly, but as the concept of such a creature; not as something to admire, but to examine; not as an object of love, but as the subject of the most complex yet scattered contemplation. And now—now I trembled in her presence, and turned pale at her approach; yet, bitterly mourning her fallen and wretched state, I remembered that she had loved

20

me for a long time, and, in a moment of poor judgment, I spoke to her of marriage.

And eventually the time of our wedding was drawing near, when one afternoon in the winter of that year—one of those unusually warm, calm, and foggy days that nurture the beautiful Halcyon (*1)—I sat (and sat, as I believed, alone) in the inner room of the library. But when I raised my eyes, I saw that Berenice was standing before me.

Was it my overactive imagination, the hazy effect of the air, the dim twilight filling the room, or the gray curtains draped around her form that made her outline seem so wavering and unclear? I couldn't determine the cause. She didn't speak a single word, and I couldn't have managed to say anything even if my life depended on it. A freezing chill swept through my body; an overwhelming sense of unbearable dread weighed down on me; an intense curiosity consumed my very being; and collapsing back into the chair, I sat there for quite some time, unable to breathe or move, my eyes locked onto her figure. Unfortunately, she had wasted away terribly, and not even the slightest trace of the person she once was remained in any part of her shape. Eventually, my intense stare shifted to her face.

The forehead was high and very pale, with an unusual calmness to it; the once jet-black hair fell partly across it, casting shadows over the sunken temples with countless curls that were now a bright yellow, clashing harshly in their strange appearance with the deep sadness that dominated the face. The eyes were lifeless and dull, appearing to have no pupils at all, and I instinctively pulled back from their glassy stare to focus instead on the thin and withered lips. They opened; and with a smile that held a strange significance, the teeth of the transformed Berenice slowly revealed themselves to me. I wish to God that I had never seen them, or that after seeing them, I had died!

The sound of a door closing startled me, and when I looked up, I discovered that my cousin had left the room. But from the chaotic chambers of my mind, the white and ghostly image of those teeth had not departed—and would not be driven away. Not a single mark on their surface—not a hint of discoloration on their enamel—not a single indentation along their edges—everything about that moment when she smiled had been burned into my memory. I could see them now even more clearly than when I had actually looked at them. The teeth!—the teeth!—they were here, there, and everywhere, visible and tangible before me; long, narrow, and extremely white, with those pale lips twisting around them, just as they had in that first terrible moment when I noticed them. Then the complete madness of my obsession took hold, and I fought uselessly against its strange and overwhelming power. Among all the countless things in the world around me, I could think of nothing but those teeth. I craved them with a frenzied longing. Everything else and all other concerns were swallowed up by my single-minded focus on them. They—and only they—filled my mind's eye, and they alone became the center of my entire mental existence. I examined them from every angle. I rotated them in every position. I studied their features. I focused on their unique qualities. I contemplated their structure. I reflected on how their nature might change. I trembled as I imagined them having feeling and awareness, and even without the lips, being capable of expressing emotion. About Mademoiselle Salle it has been rightly said, "Que tous ses pas etaient des sentiments," and about Berenice I believed even more seriously que toutes ses dents etaient des idées. Des idées!—ah, there was the insane

22

thought that ruined me! Des idées!—ah, that was why I desired them so desperately! I believed that possessing them was the only thing that could bring me peace by restoring my sanity.

And the evening closed in around me like this—and then darkness came, stayed, and left—and day broke again—and the mists of a second night were now gathering—and still I sat motionless in that lonely room—and still I sat lost in thought—and still the vision of the teeth held its terrible power over me, as it floated with the most vivid and hideous clarity among the shifting lights and shadows of the room. Finally, a cry of horror and alarm broke into my thoughts; and after a pause, this was followed by the sound of distressed voices, mixed with many quiet moans of grief or pain. I got up from my chair, and opening one of the library doors, I saw standing in the anteroom a servant girl, crying, who told me that Berenice was—dead! She had suffered an epileptic seizure early that morning, and now, as night was falling, the grave was prepared for its occupant, and all the arrangements for the burial were complete.

I found myself sitting in the library, once again sitting there alone. It felt as though I had just awakened from a confusing and disturbing dream. I knew it was now midnight, and I was fully aware that since the sun had set, Berenice had been buried. But of that grim period in between, I had no clear, or at least no definite understanding. Yet the memory was filled with horror—horror made more horrible by being unclear, and terror made more terrible by its uncertainty. It was a frightening page in the record of my existence, covered entirely with dim, hideous, and incomprehensible

23

memories. I struggled to decode them, but without success; while again and again, like the ghost of a vanished sound, the sharp and piercing scream of a woman's voice seemed to echo in my ears. I had committed an act—what was it? I asked myself the question out loud, and the whispering echoes of the room answered me,—"What was it?"

A lamp burned on the table next to me, and beside it sat a small box. There was nothing particularly special about it, and I had seen it many times before, since it belonged to our family doctor. But how had it ended up there on my table, and why did I tremble when I looked at it? I couldn't explain any of this, and eventually my gaze fell to the open pages of a book and to a sentence that had been underlined. The words were the unusual yet simple ones from the poet Ebn Zaiat: "Dicebant mihi sodales si sepulchrum amicae visitarem, curas meas aliquantulum fore levatas." So why, as I read them, did the hair on my head stand on end, and why did the blood in my body freeze in my veins?

A soft knock came at the library door, and a servant entered on tiptoe, as pale as someone from a grave. His expression was wild with terror, and he spoke to me in a voice that shook, was rough, and very quiet. What did he say? I caught only fragments of his broken sentences. He spoke of a wild scream that had shattered the night's silence, of the household gathering together, of searching in the direction where the sound had come from. Then his voice became piercingly clear as he whispered to me about a desecrated grave, about a mangled body wrapped in burial cloth, yet still breathing, still with a beating heart, still alive!

He pointed to the clothing—it was dirty and covered with dried blood. I said nothing, and he gently took my hand: it bore the marks of human fingernails pressed into the skin. He drew my attention to something against the wall. I stared at it for several minutes: it was a shovel. With a scream I leaped to the table and grabbed the box that rested on top of it. But I couldn't pry it open; and in my shaking, it slipped from my grasp and fell hard, breaking into pieces; and from it, with a clattering noise, there spilled out some dental surgery tools, mixed with thirty-two small, white and ivory-like objects that scattered across the floor in all directions.

Eleonora

Sub conservatione formæ specificæ salva anima.
    —Raymond Lully.

I come from a family known for its vivid imagination and intense emotions. People have called me insane, but the question remains unsettled whether madness represents the highest form of intelligence—whether much of what we consider magnificent—whether everything that runs deep—actually emerges from disorders of thinking—from mental states elevated at the cost of ordinary reasoning. Those who daydream are aware of many things that escape people who only dream while sleeping. In their hazy visions they catch glimpses of eternity, and feel a thrill upon waking to discover they have stood at the edge of the great mystery. In fragments, they learn something about the wisdom that comes from good, and even more about the simple knowledge that comes from evil. They venture, though without rudder or compass, into the vast ocean of "indescribable light," and once again, like the adventures of the Nubian geographer, "they dared to enter the sea of darkness, to explore what lay within it."

We will say, then, that I am insane. I admit, at least, that there are two separate states of my mental existence—the state of clear reasoning, which cannot be questioned, and which belongs to my memory of events that make up the first period of my life—and a state of uncertainty and confusion, which relates to the present, and to my recollection of what forms the second major era of my existence. Therefore, what I will tell you about the earlier period, believe; and regarding what I may share about the later time, give only the trust that seems appropriate, or doubt it completely, or, if you cannot doubt it, then solve its mystery like Oedipus.

She whom I loved in my youth, and about whom I now write calmly and clearly these memories, was the only daughter of my mother's only sister, who had long since passed away. Eleonora was my cousin's name. We had always lived together, under a tropical sun, in the Valley of the Many-Colored Grass. No wandering footstep ever entered that valley; for it lay far up among a range of enormous hills that loomed all around it, blocking the sunlight from its most beautiful hidden places. No path had been worn in the area; and, to reach our happy home, one needed to push back, with force, the leaves of thousands upon thousands of forest trees, and to crush underfoot the beauty of millions upon millions of fragrant flowers. This is how we lived completely alone, knowing nothing of the world beyond the valley—I, and my cousin, and her mother.

From the shadowy regions beyond the mountains at the far end of our enclosed valley, a narrow and deep river emerged, more brilliant than anything except Eleonora's eyes. Winding secretly through twisting paths, it eventually disappeared through a dark gorge among hills even more obscure than those from which it had come. We named it the "River of Silence" because its flow seemed to have a quieting effect. No sound came from its waters, and it moved so gently that the pearl-like stones we enjoyed watching deep within its depths remained completely still, resting peacefully in their ancient positions, gleaming magnificently for eternity.

The riverbank and the many sparkling streams that wound their way through winding paths into the main channel, along with the areas that stretched from the banks down into the depths of the water until they reached the pebbled bottom—these places, just like the entire surface of the valley from the river to the surrounding mountains, were covered with soft green grass that was thick, short, perfectly level, and scented with vanilla. The grass was scattered throughout with yellow buttercups, white daisies, purple violets, and ruby-red asphodels, and its extraordinary beauty spoke powerfully to our hearts about God's love and glory.

Throughout the grassy areas, scattered in small clusters like landscapes from dreams, extraordinary trees grew with tall, slender trunks that didn't stand straight up but leaned gracefully toward the sunlight that filtered into the center of the valley at midday. Their bark displayed a striking pattern of alternating ebony and silver stripes, smoother than anything except Eleonora's cheeks; with their massive bright green leaves spreading from the treetops in long, quivering lines that danced with the gentle breezes, one could easily imagine them as giant serpents from Syria paying tribute to their ruler, the Sun.

For fifteen years, Eleonora and I wandered hand in hand through this valley before love found its way into our hearts. It was one evening at the end of her fifteenth year and my twentieth that we sat embraced beneath the snake-like trees, gazing down at our reflections in the waters of the River of Silence. We spoke no words for the rest of that beautiful day, and even the next day our words were shaky and sparse. We had awakened the god Eros from those waters, and now we felt him ignite within us the passionate souls of our ancestors. The intense emotions that had distinguished our family for centuries came flooding back along with the imagination for which they had been equally famous, and together they breathed an intoxicating joy over the Valley of the Many-Colored Grass. Everything began to change. Strange, brilliant star-shaped flowers bloomed on trees where no flowers had ever grown before. The colors of the green ground grew deeper; and when the white daisies disappeared one by one, clusters of ruby-red asphodels sprang up in their place. Life appeared along our paths; the tall flamingo, never seen before, displayed his scarlet feathers before us alongside other bright, colorful birds. Golden and silver fish filled the river, from whose depths came a murmur that gradually grew into a soothing melody more heavenly than the music of the wind harp—sweeter than anything except Eleonora's voice. And now a massive cloud, which we had long observed in the western sky, drifted toward us in all its crimson and gold splendor, settling peacefully above us and sinking day by day until its edges touched the mountaintops, transforming their darkness into magnificence and enclosing us, as if forever, within a magical palace of grandeur and glory.

Eleonora's beauty was like that of the angels; but she was a young woman who remained simple and pure, just as her short life spent among the flowers had made her. She felt no need to hide the passionate love that filled her heart, and she shared her deepest feelings with me as we walked together through the Valley of the Many-Colored Grass, talking about the great changes that had recently happened there.

Eventually, after speaking one day with tears about the final tragic transformation that must come to all humanity, she focused exclusively on this single melancholy subject from that point forward, weaving it into every conversation we had, just as in the poetry of the bard of Shiraz, the same imagery appears repeatedly in every powerful variation of expression.

She had realized that death's mark was upon her—that, like a mayfly, she had been made perfect in beauty only to die; but her fears about the grave came from a single concern that she shared with me one evening at dusk, beside the banks of the River of Silence. She was troubled by the thought that, after burying her in the Valley of the Many-Colored Grass, I would leave forever its joyful sanctuary, giving the love that now belonged so completely to her to some woman from the ordinary world beyond. Right then and there, I threw myself quickly at Eleonora's feet and made a promise to her and to Heaven that I would never marry any woman on Earth—that I would never betray her precious memory or the devoted love with which she had blessed me. I called upon the Almighty Ruler of the Universe to witness the sacred seriousness of my promise. The curse that I asked from Him and from her, should I prove unfaithful to that vow as she became a saint in Paradise, carried a punishment so terrifyingly horrible that I cannot bring myself to record it here. Eleonora's bright eyes grew even brighter at my words; she sighed as if a crushing weight had been lifted from her chest; she trembled and wept very bitterly; but she accepted the vow (for what was she but a child?) and it brought peace to her deathbed. She told me, not many days later, as she died peacefully, that because of what I had done to comfort her spirit, she would watch over me from the spirit world when she departed, and, if it were allowed, return to me visibly during the night hours; but if this were truly beyond the power of souls in Paradise, she would at least give me frequent signs of her presence, breathing upon me in the evening breezes, or filling the air I breathed with fragrance from the angels' incense burners. With these words on her lips, she gave up her pure life, bringing the first chapter of my own to an end.

Up to this point, I have told the truth faithfully. But as I cross the barrier in Time's journey, marked by the death of my beloved, and continue with the second phase of my life, I feel that darkness gathers over my mind, and I doubt the complete sanity of this account. But let me continue.— Years dragged by heavily, and still I lived within the Valley of the Many-Colored Grass; but a second transformation had overtaken everything. The star-shaped flowers withdrew into the tree trunks and vanished completely. The colors of the green carpet grew dim; and, one after another, the ruby-red asphodels withered and died; and there grew up in their place, ten by ten, dark, eye-like violets that twisted restlessly and were always heavy with dew. And Life left our pathways; for the tall flamingo no longer displayed his scarlet feathers before us, but flew sorrowfully from the valley into the hills, along with all the bright, vibrant birds that had come with him. And the golden and silver fish swam down through the canyon at the far end of our territory and never again adorned the sweet river. And the soothing melody that had been gentler than the wind-harp of Æolus, and more heavenly than anything except the voice of Eleonora, it faded away gradually, in whispers growing quieter and quieter, until the stream returned, at last, completely, to the solemnity of its original silence. And then, finally, the massive cloud rose up, and, leaving the mountaintops to the darkness of old, retreated into the regions of Hesper, and carried away all its countless golden and magnificent glories from the Valley of the Many-Colored Grass.

However, I didn't forget Eleonora's promises; I could hear the sound of angels swinging their censers, and streams of sacred perfume constantly drifted through the valley. During solitary hours when my heart pounded heavily, the winds that cooled my forehead carried gentle sighs to me. Unclear whispers frequently filled the night air, and once— oh, just once!—I was roused from a sleep as deep as death by the touch of ghostly lips against mine.

But the emptiness in my heart still wouldn't be satisfied, even with all of this. I yearned for the love that had once filled it completely. Eventually, the valley became painful to me because of all the memories it held of Eleonora, and I abandoned it forever to pursue the shallow pleasures and chaotic victories of the world.

I found myself in a strange city, where everything seemed designed to erase from memory the sweet dreams I had cherished for so long in the Valley of the Many-Colored Grass. The splendor and ceremonies of a magnificent court, the wild clash of weapons, and the dazzling beauty of women confused and overwhelmed my mind. Yet my soul had remained faithful to its promises, and signs of Eleonora's presence still came to me during the quiet hours of the night. Suddenly these appearances stopped, and the world became dark before my eyes, and I was horrified by the burning thoughts that consumed me, by the terrible temptations that surrounded me; for there came from some distant and unknown land, into the festive court of the king I served, a young woman whose beauty immediately conquered my unfaithful heart—before whom I knelt without resistance, in the most passionate and humble worship of love. What was my passion for the young girl of the valley compared to the intensity, the madness, and the soul-lifting ecstasy of devotion with which I poured out my entire being in tears at the feet of the heavenly Ermengarde? Oh, radiant was the angel Ermengarde! and in that knowledge I had room for no other. Oh, divine was the seraph Ermengarde! and as I gazed into the depths of her unforgettable eyes, I thought only of them—and of her.

I got married—and I didn't fear the curse I had brought upon myself; its harsh consequences never came to me. And one time—just once more in the quiet of the night; the gentle sighs that had left me came through my window; and they formed themselves into a familiar and sweet voice, saying:

"Sleep peacefully! The Spirit of Love reigns and rules, and by taking Ermengarde into your passionate heart, you are absolved of your vows to Eleonora, for reasons that will be revealed to you in Heaven.

THE END

Thank You For Reading

You've Just Read a Piece of the Greatest Library Ever Rebuilt

Thank you for reading.

This book is one of thousands we're restoring, reimagining, and translating as part of the **Modern Library of Alexandria** — a global movement to preserve and share humanity's most important ideas.

What was once lost to fire and time is now rising again — not just as memory, but as living, breathing knowledge, freely accessible to all.

What You Can Do Next:

- **Keep Reading.**

  Discover more legendary works — in beautiful print, audiobook, or digital form — at LibraryofAlexandria.com.

- **Build Your Own Library.**

  Every title is available as a paperback, hardcover, or collectible boxset — at true printing cost. Craft a personal library worthy of display.

- **Spread the Light.**

  Share this book. Tell others about the movement. Help us translate every timeless work into every language, so no reader is ever left behind.

By finishing this book, you've already taken part in something extraordinary.

Join us at LibraryofAlexandria.com

Together, we're rebuilding the greatest library the world has ever known.

With appreciation,

The Modern Library of Alexandria Team

Visit:
www.libraryofalexandria.com
Or scan the code below: